The Right Note

Story by Karen Ginnane

Illustrations by Lauren McGowen

The Right Note

Text: Karen Ginnane
Publishers: Tania Mazzeo and Eliza Webb
Series consultant: Amanda Sutera
Hands on Heads Consulting
Editor: Sarah Layton
Project editor: Annabel Smith
Designer: Jess Kelly
Project designer: Danielle Maccarone
Illustrations: Lauren McGowen
Production controller: Renee Tome

NovaStar

ISBN 978 0 17 033490 7

Cengage Learning Australia
Level 5, 80 Dorcas Street
Southbank VIC 3006 Australia
Phone: 1300 790 853
Email: aust.nelsonprimary@cengage.com

For learning solutions, visit **cengage.com.au**

Printed in China by 1010 Printing International Ltd
1 2 3 4 5 6 7 29 28 27 26 25

Nelson acknowledges the Traditional Owners and Custodians of the lands of all First Nations Peoples. We pay respect to Elders past and present, and extend that respect to all First Nations Peoples today.

Contents

Chapter 1	"A Dazzling Future"	4
Chapter 2	A Filter Causes Problems	9
Chapter 3	Pa Arrives	13
Chapter 4	Wheelie-Bin Drama	16
Chapter 5	Pa Goes Missing	22
Chapter 6	What Matters Most	33
Chapter 7	Stage Fright	38
Chapter 8	110 Per Cent Nailed It!	42

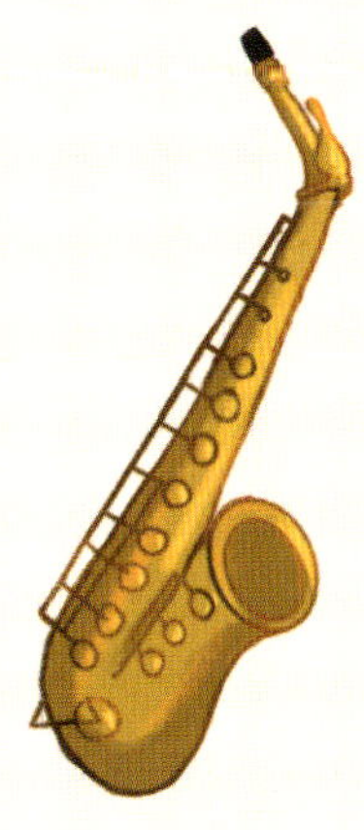

Chapter 1

"A Dazzling Future"

"Nate?"

His fingers ripple across the piano keys, to deafening applause.

"Nate!"

"These boys have a dazzling future," gushed the judge. "I have never heard such skill, such style, in musicians so young ..."

"NATE!"

Mum stood in the doorway of Nate's bedroom. "We're late for school. Quick, let's go!"

Nate snapped out of his daydream and grabbed his backpack.

Mum marched out the door and along the street up ahead, while Nate dawdled behind.

The New Jazz Competition was next week, and it was all Nate could think about. Imagine if he and Julio won the competition! Imagine the adoring crowd, the applause, the future stardom!

He and Julio would probably have to leave school for a world tour. They would single-handedly make jazz the new hip hop and fill stadiums all over the world ... how proud his Pa would be!

Nate ran to catch up with Mum. "What day does Pa get here again?" he asked.

Mum's smile was a little bit sad. "Next Wednesday, love."

"Just in time for him to come and see me and Julio take first prize in the comp!"

Mum chuckled. "You've definitely done enough piano practice! But don't get your hopes up too high, Nate – you're the youngest in the competition. Winning isn't everything, you know."

"Why not us? How many kids love jazz like we do? We're gonna absolutely, undoubtedly, 110 per cent *nail* it!"

His mum laughed out loud. "There aren't many people like you, that's for sure, Nate."

They reached the school gates and Nate could see Julio in the playground.

Mum bent to give him a kiss. "Have a good day, love."

"Bye, Mum!" He bolted through the gates, waving at Julio.

The day flew by. The last bell rang and children poured out the doors, full of Friday afternoon excitement. Nate's mum was already waiting by the gate.

Nate tugged Julio's sleeve. "Come on, Jules! We have to practise."

Julio shook his head. "I can't practise tonight. Mum says I have to go to a family dinner."

"But New Jazz is next week!" said Nate. "We have to practise every minute if we're gonna win."

Julio's expression was suddenly closed off. "Nate, you're stressing me out. This competition is everything to you."

Nate stared at his friend. "Hello? Who are you and what have you done with my music-nerd friend? Jules, you're the one who plays every spare second you've got!"

"Yeah, because it's *fun*. Because I love it! Not because I want to win some competition." Julio hoisted his bag on his shoulder. "We can practise tomorrow. See you then."

Nate trudged glumly to meet Mum. "Cheer up, kiddo," said Mum. "You're doing a video call with Pa tonight, remember?"

"Oh, yeah!" Nate brightened at the thought. They hadn't done a video call for ages – not since lockdown days during the pandemic, when they'd spent every Friday playing and listening to jazz music together from their different states. Suddenly, he couldn't wait to talk to Pa again.

Chapter 2

A Filter Causes Problems

Nate clicked on the video link and Pa was already there, waiting. Nate put on an alien filter before turning on his video.

"Take me to your leader!"

Nate giggled as Pa leaned close to the screen, his eyebrows scrunched together. "What the – Who's there? What's wrong with the computer?"

Nate burst out laughing. "Mum, come and look!"

Mum came over and took one look at Pa's confused face. "Take that filter off, *now*!" she said.

Nate took the filter off and his own bewildered face appeared on the screen. "It was a joke, Mum. I was just pranking Pa, like I always do."

Mum squeezed Nate's shoulder and bent to whisper, "I know, love, sorry. I'll explain later." She stood up and spoke brightly to the screen. "Hi, Dad! How are you? I'll leave you boys to talk jazz. Nate can't wait to show you what he's working on."

"Hello, Nathaniel, my boy," said Pa in his gravelly voice. "I hear I'm coming to see you soon?"

"I can't wait, Pa!" said Nate. "It's been so long since I've seen you! I'm practising a piece with Julio for a competition. You'll be here to see it!"

"Sorry, what's that?" Pa fiddled with his hearing aid.

"My competition piece, Pa! Me and Julio are in a jazz comp. We're doing –"

"Eh? Can't hear you properly."

"A COMPETITION, Pa. It's for –"

Pa's face was scrunched again and Nate gave up. An idea struck him. He pressed "play" on his tablet. "Listen, Pa!"

Nate leaned back and let the music flow over him, humming along. He watched Pa do the same and saw how similar their expressions were when they listened to a piece they loved. They were silent until they both tapped the closing beats together.

Nate laughed. "We're in sync, Pa!"

Pa nodded, his eyes shining. "That we are, my boy. Love you, Grandie." That was Pa's nickname for Nate.

"Love you too, Pa."

The screen went blank.

"Well, that was sudden," Nate said to himself.

"Pa finds it a bit hard to hear on devices," said Mum, making him jump. Nate hadn't heard her come back into the room. "He loses track of conversations easily these days."

She paused. “Nate, you might notice a few differences with Pa when you see him next week. He’s getting older and his memory is not what it was.”

“Is that why you got cranky about the filter?”

Mum sighed. “Yes. I’m sorry I shouted, but Pa gets mixed up easily these days and technology confuses him. We’ll *both* have to be patient. Okay?”

Chapter 3

Pa Arrives

Nate felt almost shy when Pa arrived at the airport and looked him up and down.

"Wait a minute, this isn't my little grandson. This young man probably shaves already!"

Then Pa grabbed him in a bear hug, and it was just like old times. Nate gripped Pa's arm as they headed to the car park, chattering about the competition, about Julio, about his lessons, about the book he was reading, and Pa kept nodding and smiling.

As he climbed into the backseat, with Pa and Mum in the front, Nate felt a warm rush of happiness that lasted all the way to their house.

When they arrived, Nate jumped out and opened Pa's door.

Pa looked around him, and his eyes stopped on the wheelie rubbish bins parked at the side of the house.

"I can take the bins out to the kerb for you, Jen," Pa said, pointing. "Is it bin night tonight?"

"Hmm?" said Mum, glancing around. "Oh, thanks, Dad. Bin night was yesterday, but you can do it next week. Let's get you inside, shall we?"

They went inside. Pa walked straight over to the piano and patted it, raising one eyebrow at Nate. "So, what are you playing for me?"

Nate grinned back. He came over and sat on the stool next to Pa and started to play.

Pa tilted his head, concentrating.

"Nice little tune. I seem to have heard it somewhere before ..."

Nate laughed. "Very funny, Pa! It's 'Take Five'. I played it for you last week. It's what I'm playing for the competition."

"Last week where? What competition is that, Grandie?"

"The jazz competition, Pa! I told you about it, remember –"

Mum shot Nate a look and spoke loudly. "Nate and Julio are the youngest competitors in the New Jazz Competition on Saturday, Dad! This is the piece they've been practising. They've done so well."

Nate continued playing, keeping his eyes on his fingers. The music filled the room and Pa's foot found a rhythm, tapping gently along. When Pa started to hum along, Nate sneaked a look to see Pa smiling, his expression relaxed again.

There might be some changes in Pa, thought Nate, but they would always have the music. Nate finished with an extra flourish and sat back, Pa's applause sweet in his ears.

Chapter 4

Wheelie-Bin Drama

A rumble outside his window woke Nate the next morning. He groaned. Why did the rubbish truck have to come so early?

Wait! It wasn't bin day.

Nate got up and looked out the window. Pa was dragging one of the wheelie bins, dressed in just slippers and the tracksuit he wore as pyjamas.

But it was the wrong time and the wrong day. He must have forgotten what Mum said.

The clock read 4.48 am. It was too early to worry about bins, or anything else. Nate climbed back into bed and stuck his head under the pillow.

♫

"Mum! I can't find my new runners!"

"You left them in the hall – they were still in the box," called Mum.

"They're not there now," said Nate. "MUM!"

"Then just wear your old ones today!" said Mum. "They'll be somewhere."

"But I need them," Nate complained.

Mum huffed impatiently. "For goodness' sake, Nate. Those runners are for the competition – you don't need them today. Have you had breakfast yet?"

"Yeah, I've been awake for hours," groaned Nate. He hadn't gone back to sleep after his unwelcome wheelie-bin alarm clock.

"How come?" asked Mum.

"Nothing. Well, something ..." He shot a look at Pa reading in his armchair and lowered his voice. "Pa took the bins out to the kerb really early."

"What?" said Mum. "Oh. Well, I'll just have to bring them back in, I guess." She shrugged. "Get ready and I'll see you out the front."

Nate put on his old shoes, grabbed his bag and ran outside. His mum had pulled the overflowing wheelie bin off the footpath.

"What on Earth has he put in this?" she said, flipping the lid up. "They were only emptied yesterday."

There, on top of various household items, was a brand-new shoebox.

"My runners!" Nate grabbed the box. "He threw my new runners in the bin!"

"Oh dear," said Mum. "He must have thought the box was rubbish. I'll have to go through these bins when I get back."

Nate tucked the box safely out of sight on the front porch and ran back. "But you can tell there's shoes inside as soon as you pick it up!" he said.

They started to walk to school. “I know, love,” said Mum. “Pa’s not making sense of things the way he used to. He’s got something called Alzheimer’s disease.”

It rhymes with “old timers”, thought Nate. “What’s that?”

“It’s a disease that older people can get sometimes. It causes something called dementia. It makes them forget things they once knew. They can get confused about where they are and what’s happening around them.” Mum took a deep breath. “It’s difficult to see people we love change, isn’t it? But he’s still your wonderful Pa. That’s one thing that won’t change, Nate.”

Nate was unusually quiet as he walked home with Julio after school. Pa was watching them from the porch.

“Hi, Mr Melville!” called Julio.

Pa peered at Julio. “Who’s this young man?” he asked. “Is that you, Bertie?”

Julio laughed. “I’m not Bertie – it’s me, Julio!”

“My best friend from school,” said Nate quickly, seeing the expression on Pa’s face. “He’s the one who’s really good at sax, remember?”

“Of course he remembers,” said Julio. “He gave me that old Ravi Coltrane record last time he was over.”

"We've both grown a lot; we look different," said Nate defensively. He felt strangely nervous talking about Pa's disease – even with his best friend.

As soon as the boys started to practise their song in the lounge room, Nate relaxed. He could see Pa settle into the music as well.

Later that evening, Nate heard Pa talking to Mum in the kitchen. "It was good to see Bertie again after all these years."

"Bertie?" asked Mum.

"You know, Bertie. The Italian kid, Umberto. We went to school together."

"Oh, I see." She obviously didn't see. "Did you see an old photo of him or something?" asked Mum.

"He was here, Jenny! Very good on the sax now, too," said Pa.

"Ah," said Mum. "That was Julio, Dad. Nate's school friend."

"Yes, my school friend. That's what I said. Nice to see him again."

"That's good, Dad." But the feeling in Mum's voice didn't match her words.

Chapter 5

Pa Goes Missing

The day of the competition was already warm at 7 am. Nate was up and dressed, pacing around the kitchen.

"Nate, you don't have to be ready for over an hour yet," said Mum, still in her dressing gown.

"I couldn't sleep," said Nate. His stomach was fluttering with butterflies.

"Nerves are normal," said Mum. She tousled his hair. "I'm going to take a shower. Deep breaths, okay?"

But it wasn't just the performance Nate was worried about – it was Julio.

Yesterday they had run through their piece a couple of times and made a few mistakes – just little things, nothing to worry about.

Nate had wanted to run through the song one last time, but Julio had grabbed his sax and shoved it into its case.

"You don't get it, do you?" Julio had snapped. "You've never doubted yourself in your entire life!" He'd stormed out.

Nate had messaged him afterwards, but Julio still hadn't replied.

"Nate, can you get some breakfast for you and Pa, please?" called Mum.

At least getting some food would give him something else to think about. Nate got the plates out and took the butter out of the fridge to soften. He went into the hallway and tapped on Pa's door.

"Cup of tea, Pa?" No answer. Was he still asleep? Nate tapped on the bedroom door again and pushed it open a crack. "Pa?"

Still no answer. Nate pushed the door wide. The bedroom was empty.

Nate frowned. Was Pa out in the garden? A quick scout around the front and back of the house proved that he wasn't. He wasn't in any of the other rooms in the house, either.

Nate's stomach started to squirm with something more than butterflies.

"Mum?" he shouted. "Pa's gone!"

Mum ran into Pa's room seconds later, hair dripping wet from the shower.

"He's left his phone and his wallet!" She pressed her hands to her temples. "Think, Jenny! Nate, I need you to run around the block and look for him. And check the shops and cafes, okay? I'm calling your dad."

Nate took off, glad to have somewhere to go. It was already hot in the sun. As he ran, he turned left and right to check front yards and laneways as he passed. He ran inside the local store, squinting in the suddenly dim light, but no Pa. He broke into a sprint. By the time he got back to the house, he was sweating.

Mum was on the phone on the front porch. She hung up when she saw Nate. "Anything?"

"He's nowhere," Nate replied.

A car door slammed nearby, and they turned to see Nate's dad running up the street. "Have you found him?" Dad called.

"No! He could be lost, and we can't track him because he doesn't have his phone." Mum looked distraught.

"Have you called the police?" asked Dad.

"Yes, and all the neighbours." Mum scrolled through her phone. "I'm putting a message on the neighbourhood social media page now," she said, tapping her screen furiously.

"I'm looking for a recent photo – oh, here's one. Can I use this, Nate?"

It was a picture of Nate with Pa's arm around him. Nate swallowed the lump in his throat and nodded quickly.

Mum pressed “send”. “Okay, that’s posted. I’ve added my contact details.” She showed them the screen. “Someone needs to stay at the house in case he comes back or if the police come.”

Dad was clenching his jaw the way he did when he was stressed. “You stay here, Jen. I’m going to drive around and keep looking. I’ll take Nate.”

Mum nodded, her eyes watery. Dad gave her a hug. “Don’t worry. We’ll find him.”

He ran back to his car, Nate close behind.

Only they didn't find him. They drove round and round, stopping the car every so often so Nate could run in and check a shop, a cafe, a neighbour's house – but Pa was nowhere to be seen.

The time that they needed to leave for the competition came and went, and still no Pa. Disappointment squirmed like a worm in Nate's gut, but he pushed it down. It was only a small worm, compared to the terrible python of dread he felt thinking about his beloved Pa, lost and maybe not okay.

After what seemed like hours, Dad pulled up in the supermarket car park. “Pa will be dehydrated in this heat,” said Dad, handing Nate some cash. “You’d better get some water for when we find him.”

But Nate heard an “if” behind Dad’s “when”.

The cold frosting on the bottle had already disappeared by the time Nate climbed back into the front seat. Dad started to drive out of the car park, past the supermarket rubbish bins.

Realisation struck Nate like a physical blow.

“Wait!” he shouted. “The bins!” He pointed at a gap between the bins, bouncing in his seat in excitement. “One of them’s missing! That’s what we have to look for.”

Dad had slammed the brakes hard at Nate's shout. "What on Earth! What are you talking about, Nate?"

"Pa loves wheelie bins! He told me he wanted one of these big ones for Mum when we drove past some coming back from the airport. If we find the missing bin, we'll find Pa – I just know it!"

Dad shook his head. "Those things are huge, Nate. If Pa could even move one, he can't have gone far."

"Pa has the strength of a superhero when it comes to wheelies, Dad."

Nate looked around, scanning the park on the other side of the road. "There! By the lake! I can see him."

Dad looked where Nate was pointing. "Bingo! You're right, Nate." He accelerated across the road and pulled up next to the park. "Quick, run! I'll park the car and follow."

Nate jumped out of the car and bolted towards Pa, who was making his slow way along the path that circled the lake, hauling an enormous wheelie bin behind him.

Some curious adults hovered nearby, watching. One was tapping on her phone.

"Pa. Pa! Wait for me," called Nate. "PA!"

Pa looked around in confusion before catching sight of Nate. He waved. "Nate, come and give me a hand. We need to get this back to your mum."

Nate caught up with Pa, whose face was covered in sweat. He was still wearing his pyjama tracksuit. "Pa, it's too hot! Come and sit in the shade. I've got some water."

Pa looked around suspiciously. “Pa, no one’s going to take the bin!” Nate said. He took Pa’s arm and led him to a bench under a tree by the lake.

The woman who’d been on her phone came over. “Is this your missing Pa? I tried to help, but he waved me away.”

Nate opened the bottle of water and gave it to Pa, who drank thirstily. “Yes, this is my Pa – wait. How did you know?”

“Your mum’s post on the neighbourhood social page went viral,” said the woman, showing Nate her phone.

Dad came running across the grass, panting. “I’ve called Mum,” he said, “and the police are on their way.”

Nate knew there was no point in asking, but he asked anyway. “What time is it, Dad?”

Dad shook his head sadly. “You’re meant to be on stage now, Nate. I’m so sorry, buddy.”

Chapter 6

What Matters Most

Nate had missed his big chance.

He had to blink hard before the park came back into focus.

But then Nate looked at his Pa, who was looking back at him with his kind, brown eyes. He imagined him labouring in this hot sun, pulling a bin he was sure they needed, because he loved them.

He remembered his Pa playing him his jazz records, singing along with his wonderful, deep voice.

He realised he couldn't even think of music without immediately thinking of Pa. Music and his Pa were always connected in his head.

Nate loved jazz music because of his Pa – but he loved his Pa more.

If Nate had to choose between playing in front of the biggest audience in the world and making sure his Pa was safe, he knew what he would choose.

It was the same choice that they'd made today, and he didn't regret it – not for one minute. There would be many other days to play music, but there might not be many more days to be with Pa.

Nate sat down next to Pa on the bench. "Tell me about the time you first heard live jazz again, Pa," he said.

Pa's face brightened, and Nate could see him looking back at treasured memories. "Ah. I was only sixteen," began Pa, his eyes bright and clear as he told the story Nate had heard many times before.

Pa finished his story and looked proudly at Nate. "And now you can play like that. Your music makes me very happy, Grandie."

The park went blurry again as Nate blinked back tears – but this time, he was smiling. "Come on, Pa. Let's go home and play some jazz."

A siren wailed and a police car pulled up next to the park, blue lights strobing. Mum jumped out and came running over, two police officers behind her. She sat down close to Pa and looked searchingly at his face.

"Dad, you're okay! Oh, Dad! You had us so worried." She burst into tears and flung her arms around him.

Pa patted her leg awkwardly. "Oh, dear, what a fuss about nothing, Jen!" He winked at Nate. "Just having a yarn with my best mate here."

Another car pulled up behind the police car and Julio tumbled out, his parents close behind. He ran up to Nate. “Is your Pa okay, Nate?”

Nate looked at Julio and realised that his friend knew about his Pa’s illness. Perhaps Julio’s parents had told him? But there was nothing to feel nervous about, thought Nate. In fact, it was a huge relief that his best friend finally knew the truth. He smiled at Julio. “Yes, he’s fine, thanks.”

Julio looked at Nate. "I'm really sorry about the competition, Nate. I know how important it was to you."

Nate shrugged. "It's OK. We can't do anything –"

He stopped mid-sentence, looking over at Julio's mum. She was waving frantically at them from the car, mobile in hand.

"Boys! They've rearranged your slot! You're on last – we can still make it!"

Nate leapt to his feet. "What? Really?"

"What?" said Julio, with a very different tone.

"Quick! We have to go now!" she called.

Nate looked frantically at Mum. "Can you all come?"

"I need to get Pa home and make sure he's okay, Nate," said Mum. "But I promise we'll come as fast as we can after that!"

"Sounds like you boys will need a police escort if you're going to make it to your concert without breaking the law," said one officer. "We'll take you, if your parents agree."

Chapter 7

Stage Fright

At any other time, being driven in a police car with the siren blaring and cars pulling out of their way would have been the highlight of Nate's year. It was still a buzz, but seeing Julio sitting pale and silent next to him took the shine off the moment.

Also, the fact that they'd had to leave without Pa and his parents – but especially Pa.

"What's wrong, Jules?" he asked, yet again, but Julio just shook his head and hunched even further into himself.

"We're gonna make it, don't worry. And we'll be good when we get up on stage – you'll see. Nerves are normal. The butterflies in my tummy are like eagles!"

It was true. Nate's stomach was churning, but he knew that as soon as they played that first note, they'd forget everything but the music.

The police car screeched to a halt in front of the huge town hall and the boys tumbled out, shouting thanks to the officers sitting in the car beneath the blue lights.

They ran inside and Nate quickly explained the situation to an organiser. Another woman led them backstage, which was a jumble of instruments, cables, equipment and nervously milling musicians. Another woman holding a clipboard came forward.

"Nate and Julio?" she asked in a stage whisper. They nodded.

"Your timing is perfect," she said with a wink. "You're on in five minutes. Get yourselves ready, please."

Julio unclipped his saxophone case and Nate peered out from the wings to look at the piano on stage. He gasped.

The hall was huge, and it was jam-packed. The stage lights meant that the faces and bodies below them were in darkness, but Nate could sense hundreds of pairs of eyes trained on the stage, looking towards where they would be performing.

Nate stepped back and let out a breath. "Wow," he whispered. They had never played anywhere remotely like this. The quartet before them were brilliant, and their closing notes raised cheers and applause.

Nate closed his eyes and took deep breaths, as his teacher had taught him. The moment was here.

He opened his eyes and turned to Julio. "It's you and me, buddy," he whispered.

But Julio had frozen, staring at the stage and audience. His pupils were huge, like a terrified animal. "I – I can't. I just can't –"

Julio backed away from the stage, clutching his sax and shaking his head.

Nate heard the MC announce, "Nate Melville and Julio Moltoni, our youngest performers, will round off our program today. Please give them your very warmest welcome!"

The woman with the clipboard was talking gently to Julio, but he kept shaking his head, looking petrified. She patted his arm and gestured to another woman, who led Julio away.

The woman turned back to Nate. "Your poor friend is having a panic attack. Can you play this piece by yourself?"

No, he couldn't. He needed Julio for the melody. But he heard himself say, "Yes, I can."

Chapter 8

110 Per Cent Nailed It!

Nate walked onto the brightly lit stage, the lights blinding him. A bead of sweat ran down the back of his neck as the applause slowed. He adjusted the microphone and cleared his throat, trying to remember the introduction he'd practised so many times. He had planned to be cool as a cucumber – totally chill.

"Um. My name is Nate Melville, and this is Julio – I mean. Julio isn't. He can't ... um." He stammered to a stop and the silence rang loud in his ears. "So, it's just me playing 'Take Five' by Paul Desmond in the Dave Brubeck Quartet. It's my Pa's favourite piece."

Well, that was really cool, Nate, he thought.

In the quiet of the hushed room, a movement at the back of the hall caught his eye. Three people were being ushered in and now that his eyes had adjusted to the lighting, he could see that they were his mum, dad and Pa. They'd made it – but in this moment, Nate wished they hadn't.

Then, into that awful, waiting silence, he heard Pa call out. "Make me proud, Grandie!"

But Nate knew that Pa was going to watch him fail. He was so small, and this audience was so big. How had he thought he could do justice to one of the most famous jazz classics on his own?

He couldn't do it.

He *had* to do it.

Nate sat down very slowly at the piano. He'd have to adjust his performance to include the melody that Julio would normally play on the sax.

His fingers felt like claws on the keyboard. He started the piece, but his fingers hit the wrong key. Flustered, he stopped. Started again. His heart was thudding so hard that he couldn't hear anything else.

His mouth was sticky and dry, as if the hot lights had sucked all the moisture from his body. It was hard even to breathe. There was just a blank in his head where the notes should be. The silence was too loud and much too long.

He'd lost the song. He'd lost it!

And then, the melody washed over him.

But these were not his notes. These soft, calming, beautiful notes were drifting from the side of the stage.

Nate turned and looked into the wings. Julio stood behind the curtain, playing the melody that Nate had lost. Playing it perfectly, as if there was no other way to play it.

Nate took a deep breath and the song came rushing back to him. His hands finally remembered how to play the music. He kept his eyes on Julio, and Julio looked at Nate until slowly, Julio stepped forward, one foot after the other.

Then, he was on stage next to Nate. The two boys smiled at each other, Nate holding the rhythm for Julio's melody. His relief washed into the music, and it didn't even matter if they missed the odd note – they just flowed on.

Nate quietened for Julio's solo and Julio played as Nate had never heard him play before. His best friend absolutely, undoubtedly, 110 per cent nailed it.

The audience cheered and whistled as Julio lowered his sax and Nate started his own solo. This time, the notes found his fingers, not the other way around. He looked out into the audience and found his Pa and smiled at him.

This is for you, Pa, Nate thought, and he poured all the love and sadness he felt into one minute of piano.

By the end of his solo, the bright lights were a bit blurry, but that was okay. There was a long silence from the audience.

Nate saw a man at the front hastily wipe his eyes. And then, the room erupted.

The crowd surged to their feet in a standing ovation that drowned out their final notes, but it didn't matter. Mum and Dad were standing, as was Pa, and Nate could see them clapping and smiling and wiping their eyes, too.

Nate stood up and hugged Julio awkwardly around the sax.

"Thanks for saving my life, Jules," said Nate.

"You saved me!" said Julio. "When I saw you out there, living my very worst nightmare – it made me forget about my own fear. I couldn't just leave you there."

The boys turned back to the audience, arms still around each other, and took a bow.

It didn't even matter if they came first, second or last, Nate realised. Whatever the results of the competition, Nate knew that today they'd both

absolutely,

undoubtedly,

110 per cent

won!